Big Dream Treehouses:

Using The 80/20 Rule!

Marcy Schaaf

When I was a child, my father, Charlie Schaaf, shared a powerful lesson with me that has stayed with me all my life. He told me to always focus on what truly matters—the things I'm passionate about, the dreams that light me up. This advice helped me achieve many of my own goals, and now I want to share that wisdom with you.

In Timmy's Big Dream: The Treehouse Builder, you'll follow Timmy as he learns to focus on his big dream, even when it seems like he doesn't have enough tools, time, or support. Through hard work and staying true to his vision, Timmy turns his dream into reality. This story is about more than just building a treehouse—it's about believing in yourself, following your passions, and learning that with focus and determination, anything is possible. I hope you enjoy Timmy's journey and that it inspires you to follow your own dreams, just as my father's advice inspired me.

Timmy loved dreaming big, but he had one huge dream—building a treehouse!

There was only one problem: Timmy had
no money, no tools, and no wood.

One day, he saw an ad in the local newspaper—free wood pallets!

The store was giving them away, and Timmy got an idea!

Every day, after school,
he asked for one pallet.

The store owner gave him a pallet, happy
to help.

Timmy dragged each pallet home and
took it apart.

Timmy used his allowance to buy a hammer at a neighbor's garage sale.

He now had tools and wood, nails but
no paint.

He asked around, and someone donated leftover paint!

Timmy was excited—his dream was coming together slowly.

He started
hammering,
building his
treehouse piece by
piece.

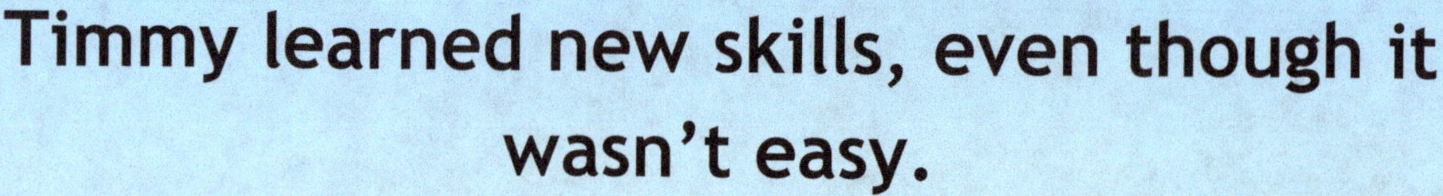

Timmy learned new skills, even though it wasn't easy.

Some friends said,
"Why not just play
like us?"

But Timmy smiled, "I'm working on something special!"

Some kids laughed.
"That'll never
work!" they said.

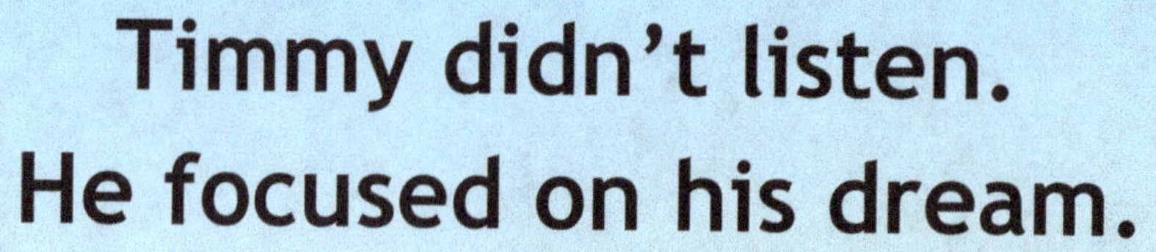

Timmy didn't listen.
He focused on his dream.

The kids who believed in him started cheering him on!

Timmy worked for weeks, using
every piece of wood he could find.

His treehouse took shape, and it
was better than he ever imagined!

At last, Timmy had built the
treehouse of his dreams.

As time went on, Timmy realized he
was good at building things.

People started asking him to build
treehouses for them!

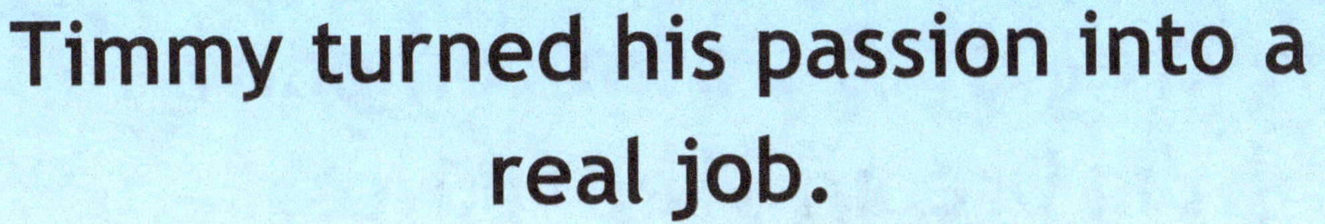

Timmy turned his passion into a
real job.

He created his own company,
Big Dream Treehouses!

Now, Timmy builds amazing treehouses for kids everywhere.

There are a few companies and organizations that offer free treehouse plans, though many focus on providing basic designs or resources to get started:

The Treehouse Guide: While not a company, this site provides free downloadable plans and comprehensive guides for treehouse building. Their free plans include simple platforms and detailed building tips, with some more advanced designs available for purchase.

MyOutdoorPlans: This website offers several free treehouse plans, including basic playhouses and elevated platforms, along with material lists and construction diagrams. Their plans are straightforward and suitable for DIY builders

Mother Earth News does indeed offer resources for building treehouses!
They provide a variet
y of articles and guides that include tips on designing and constructing treehouses, along with safety considerations and materials needed. While some of their resources may not be full-fledged plans, they offer valuable insights and advice to help DIY builders.

Notable Resources from Mother Earth News:
How to Build a Treehouse: This article outlines essential considerations for planning and building a treehouse, including safety tips, materials, and design ideas .

Treehouse Living: This section features custom, eco-friendly treehouse options and could inspire creative designs .
You can explore their website for detailed guides and articles on treehouse construction, which may serve as a helpful foundation for your project.

Join Our Book of the Month Club!

Looking for the perfect gift that keeps on giving? Join our Book of the Month Club! For just $25 a month, or $250 if you purchase a year upfront, you or your loved ones will receive a handpicked children's book every month, straight to your doorstep.

Here's how it works:
Choose from 15 different languages to receive bilingual books that make learning fun.
Enjoy monthly shipments of our exclusive books that inspire, teach, and entertain children of all ages.
Each month's book is carefully selected to provide a new adventure, valuable lesson, and a chance to explore cultures from around the world.
It's the perfect gift for birthdays, holidays, or just because! Whether you're nurturing a young reader or encouraging language learning, our Book of the Month Club is designed to bring joy to every bookshelf.

Exclusive Bonus: As part of your membership, you'll also receive a monthly podcast about our featured book delivered straight to your email! Listen in for behind-the-scenes insights, fun facts, and tips for making storytime even more magical.

Sign up today at www.Booksbyschaaf.com and start enjoying the gift of reading all year long!

Books By Schaaf

www.BookBySchaaf.com

Find us at:

www.ingramcontent.com/pod-product-compliance
Lightning Source LLC
Chambersburg PA
CBHW080819120726
48001CB00009B/2945